GEOFFREY KICHENSIDE

BRITISH RAIL
IN ACTION

DAVID & CHARLES
NEWTON ABBOT LONDON NORTH POMFRET (VT)
VANCOUVER

ISBN 0 7153 7427 3

Library of Congress Catalog Card Number 77-89375

Photoset in 10 on 11 Times
printed and bound in Great Britain by
Redwood Burn Limited
Trowbridge & Esher
for David & Charles (Publishers) Limited
Brunel House Newton Abbot Devon

Published in the United States of America
by David & Charles Inc
North Pomfret Vermont 05053 USA

Published in Canada
by Douglas David & Charles Limited
1875 Welch Street North Vancouver BC

CONTENTS

Frontispiece: A summer Saturday audience for Class 50 No 50 002 as it passes Sydney Gardens, Bath, with the 14.15 Paddington–Bristol train on 5 July 1975.

P J Fowler

INTRODUCTION

As British Railways gradually expand into the 200km/hr (125mph) era it seems hard to realise that we have had a decade not only in which steam trains have not been seen in ordinary service on British Railways but one which has seen the completion of so many aspects of modernisation schemes that have changed the face of many routes both in visual appearance and in operation. It is just on 20 years since the first diesel locomotives built under the 1955 modernisation plan took to the rails and since that time many classes have come and gone. As this book was in preparation the last of the Western Region diesel-hydraulic classes, the Westerns—which actually acquired an enthusiast following in their last years much as steam locomotives had done before them—were finally being withdrawn, so that today diesel traction on the WR bears no resemblance to that of the early 1960s. On other parts of BR nearly all the smaller diesel classes have been withdrawn as non-standard, some less than 10 years old. Moreover, with reductions in traffic, combined with reshuffling of the diesel fleet following completion of the electrification between London and Glasgow in 1974, and the introduction of the new high-speed trains, 'Inter-city 125', between Paddington, Bristol and South Wales in 1976, a start has been made on the withdrawal of some of the earlier standard classes, for example the British Railways-built Type 2s with Sulzer engines, now forming Class 24. At the same time a new class of locomotive was introduced to BR in 1976, the new Class 56 which externally looks very much like the Brush Class 47s but is equipped with the present-day development of the English Electric V16 diesel engine, nominally rated at 3,500hp. In practice British Rail will operate it at a slightly lower power but, nevertheless, the Class 56s and the Deltic locomotives on the East Coast main line are the two most powerful diesel classes on BR today.

The Deltic locomotives themselves, which work the principal expresses between Kings Cross, Leeds, Newcastle and Edinburgh, were specially designed for high-speed service and were the first to be approved for 100mph running on BR. They were developed from the prototype locomotive built by English Electric to demonstrate advantages of high horse power during the late 1950s and the prototype Deltic can be seen today preserved in the Science Museum in London. The 22 production Deltics on the East Coast main line are specially rostered to the fastest services but the new Class 56 locomotives have been designed right from the start for heavy freight haulage as much as anything else, although they will be capable of undertaking limited passenger work if needed, although future Inter-city passenger developments in the 1980s will be with the 125mph high-speed trains and the even more revolutionary advanced passenger trains, and the motive power for passenger and freight will gradually become far more segregated than today. The new Class 56 locomotives, the first 30 of which have been built in Rumania, are likely to be built in increasing numbers as a standard class and will allow the withdrawal of the older classes as they fall due for major repairs.

Although all these developments with new types of power are gradually getting under way now and will ultimately lead to far more standardisation than has been the case in the first years of diesel and electric traction, there is still plenty of variety to be seen around the British Rail network. Some diesel classes are still confined to certain areas or regions, for example the Class 33s of the Southern which because of their equipment and capability for working in conjunction with Southern electric units are based entirely at Southern Region depots. Similarly, the Deltics as we have already seen are broadly confined to the East Coast main line and the Class 50s largely to Western Region passenger services between London and South Wales, Bristol and Penzance. In contrast, the Brush Class 47 locomotives can be found on all regions, although they are not allocated to the Southern but work through on certain inter-regional passenger and freight trains.

Even electrified lines have their variety as each succeeding batch of new stock differs from its predecessors. The Southern Region, with its network of third rail electric services presents a vastly different picture from the West Coast main line, electrified on the high voltage ac overhead system with its 100mph locomotive-hauled trains, and the newly electrified suburban routes from Kings Cross and Moorgate. The latter route has been equipped with new trains, but some of the designs are based on earlier types of train used on outer suburban services from Euston and originally built in 1966. The new trains for the inner-suburban services from Moorgate which run underground for part of their journey have been developed from an experimental train of sliding door stock which has been on trial on the Southern Region and known as the 4PEP type. Regrettably these new trains entered service just after the preparatory work on this book had been completed, too late for photographers to take full advantage of them in service. The new Inter-city 125 units working from Paddington however were introduced just in time for some striking photographs to be taken in varying locations, and showing the impressive front-end design of the power cars. They contrast vividly with the older types of diesel, for example the English Electric Class 40, the first BR production diesel type to be used on express passenger work in 1957. Part of the front-end of the Inter-city 125 units shows the design treatment that has been necessary to combat a major and very worrying trend in Britain, that of vandalism, for the driver's front window has been made as small as possible and with very tough glass to resist objects hitting the front of the cab at speed. Indeed, the menace of obstructions being placed in front of trains with possible injury or death to train crews, and to the people doing it, is now so great in some areas that BR is taking special measures to catch those responsible before they injure themselves and people on the trains.

This album presents many aspects of British Rail today, in good action photographs portraying many types of locomotives currently in service in as many locations as possible. In assembling the photographs my thanks are due to all those photographers who have contributed to the book and who are credited individually for their work.

GMK

DELTICS TO SCOTLAND

ne 22 3300hp Deltic locomotives of the East Coast main ne introduced in 1961 are intensively used and arranged n duties covering the principal expresses between Kings ross, Leeds, Newcastle and Edinburgh. All are named nd carry the names of racehorses or army regiments.

Still at the time the photograph was taken, on 18 March 1970, carrying its original number D9017 and in green livery, the locomotive which is today 55 017 *The Durham Light Infantry* eases round the curves leaving King Edward bridge and heads up the East Coast main line soon after starting with the 14.11 Newcastle–Kings Cross.

K Groundwater

Above: Bearing its two white-spot headlights in place of its four-character headcode indicator, No 55 007 *Pinza* leaves Kings Cross with the 12.10 to Aberdeen on 12 April 1976.   *K Connolly*

Left: Class 55 No 9018 *Ballymoss* eases out of Edinburgh Waverley with the up Flying Scotsman for Kings Cross on 13 May 1972.   *G T Heavyside*

Below: Doncaster continues to play an important role as a major junction, not only for passenger services on the East Coast main line but also for trains to Leeds and Hull, and for freight between industrial Humberside and the collieries and other industry of South Yorkshire. Here Class 55 No 9008 *The Green Howards* passes Doncaster with an up express for Kings Cross on 29 May 1972.   *G T Heavyside*

Above: Although York has lost many of its local and cross-country services it is still an important junction between the East Coast main line, West Yorkshire and the Scarborough line. The station was built on a curved site and non-stopping expresses must slow to about 15mph to take the curves safely. No 55 010 *The King's Own Scottish Borderer* eases into the curve with a Kings Cross–Edinburgh train on 16 August 1975. *K Connolly*

Right: With an exhaust that would do justice to any steam locomotive No 55 013 *The Black Watch* accelerates up the climb between Gasworks and Copenhagen tunnels soon after leaving Kings Cross, on 24 August 1974. *Paul Clarke*

Below: A gathering of Deltics at the refuelling sidings at Kings Cross. *K Connolly*

2 ELECTRICS ON THE WEST COAST ROUTE

The West Coast main line has been electrified in stages starting with Manchester and Liverpool and gradually extended to London and more recently to Glasgow between 1960 and 1974. Seven basic classes of electric locomotive are used with the latest built in 1973/4, the Class 87 of 5000hp, being the most powerful single unit locomotive on BR. All can run at 100mph but none except No 87 001 *Stephenson* is named.

Top left: Departure line-up at Euston on 16 March 1975 with, on the left, Class 86 No E3160 still carrying its old number, and No 86 045.　　*Barry J Nicolle*

Bottom left: A Class 85 electric locomotive climbs the down carriage line through Park Street tunnels just outside Euston, with an empty train bound for Willesden carriage depot on 6 March 1973.　　*P A Dobson*

Below: Up and down expresses pass one another at the top of Camden bank about a mile out of Euston. A Class 86 heads the approaching 12.50 Euston–Liverpool. The two tracks between the trains are electrified on both the 25,000V ac overhead system and the 630V dc third rail system and are used both by ac electric trains and by the dc Euston–Watford local trains.　　*D Griffiths*

Left: Class 87 005 eases slightly as it approaches the
50mph speed restriction for the reverse curves at Berk-
hamsted with a Liverpool–Euston train on 26 May 1975.
Note the cross-arm pantograph with which this class of
locomotive is fitted. *Kevin Lane*

Bottom left: At one time BR intended to continue the func-
tion of Bletchley as an important junction between the
Cambridge and Oxford lines and the West Coast main line.
A scheme was evolved whereby freight from the East
Coast main line at Sandy, and the West Coast main line,
for destinations south of London would be routed from
Bletchley via Oxford and Reading. A new flyover was built
to keep the freight out of the way of high-speed express
passenger trains but the scheme as a whole came to
nothing and the flyover is used today only by a few parcels
and empty trains. A Class 86 electric locomotive passes
with a down express in August 1970. *D E Canning*

Below: Birmingham New Street station was extensively
rebuilt as part of the major modernisation carried out there
in connection with electrification. A large shopping area
was incorporated into the design. The trains now run to
platforms underneath the new development, which to
passengers looks for all the world like an underground station. Electric locomotive No 86 034 waits to leave for
Euston with an express while a Class 310 four-car outer
suburban electric multiple-unit waits to work a semi-fast
service to Euston on 12 June 1975. *J G Glover*

ft: For some unaccountable reason BR does not recog-
se the publicity value of naming locomotives other than
e few that received names some years ago. Although at
st none of the LMR's electric locomotives received
ames the BRB relented in the case of No 87 001 which
as named *Stephenson* to mark the 150th anniversary of
e Stockton & Darlington Railway in 1975. Here 87 001
ters Crewe with a Euston–Liverpool train on 2 May
976. *K Connolly*

ottom left: Class 87 015 brakes as it passes Stafford on
e through lines to take the 60mph speed limit round the
rve at Queensville just south of the station with a
asgow–Euston train on 27 November 1975.
K Connolly

Below: Class 85 No 85 006 accelerates away from Crewe
up the West Coast main line with a parcels train on 22
November 1975. *K Connolly*

Above left: The roadbuilders in constructing the M6 motorway followed the alignment of the West Coast main line through the Lune Gorge on the climb towards Shap, where No 87 007 speeds towards Tebay with the 14.05 from Birmingham New Street to Glasgow and Edinburgh on 11 May 1974. It is a sobering thought that much of the freight carried by road today on the M6 could be conveyed on that newly electrified railway. For a Saturday afternoon the motorway seems remarkably deserted.

G T Heavyside

Bottom left: Unless troubled by wet rails or leaves on the line, today's electrics speed up Shap as though it was virtually level, a remarkable contrast to the days of steam. No 86 236 heads towards Shap summit with a down relief passenger train for Glasgow on 26 June 1976. A problem which has become apparent since the line was electrified is the havoc that can be caused to the overhead catenary by high winds, and additional masts and supports have been erected on exposed sections of line which can be seen here alternating with the original masts of a darker shade. This photograph also makes an interesting comparison with one taken in the identical location in the 1890s which appears on page 68 of *The West Coast Route to Scotland*, also published by David & Charles.

G T Heavyside

Above: The West Coast route electric locomotives are equally at home on passenger and freight services, although occasionally with wet rail they have problems with wheel slip in climbing the steep gradients over Shap and Beattock summits. Here No 85 039 heads out of Mossend yard near Glasgow with a heavy freight for Carlisle on 24 April 1974, a few weeks before the final inauguration of the full electric passenger timetable between London and Glasgow.

M Bryce

THE CLASS 47s—BR's ALL-PURPOSE DIESEL

e 2750hp Brush Type 4, now known as Class 47,
merically is BR's largest main line diesel class and can
found working in all regions, although appearances on
e Southern are confined to inter-regional through work-
gs. Their maximum speed of 95mph can cope with most
ter-city services and they are used turn and turn about
freight, passenger and parcels workings.

bove: Class 47 naming ceremony!   *P J Fowler*

op left: A Class 47 accelerates away from Bristol past
ctoria Park on the morning of 14 May 1976 with the
irling—Newton Abbot car sleeper train. This train is
pular not only with Scottish holidaymakers visiting the
est Country but also with visitors from Devon and Corn-
all to Scotland.   *P J Fowler*

ottom left: Berkshire blizzard with Class 47 No 1651
assing Midgham with the up Cornish Riviera Express on
February 1971.   *D E Canning*

Above: The Class 47s reach the far west of Cornwall for there are no restrictions over the Royal Albert bridge such as those which barred the King Class 4-6-0s of the Great Western from reaching Cornish tracks. No 1718 eases round the curves off the Royal Albert bridge over the River Tamar and crosses from Cornwall into Devon as it approaches the suburbs of Devonport with the 13.15 Penzance–Paddington on 24 June 1973.   *C Plant*

Top right: Even though the West Coast main line is electrified, diesel locomotives are still used on a number of freight services; Class 47 No 1830 heads a train of car components vans and other freight for North Thameside and is seen here heading south from Crewe near Madeley on 16 June 1972.   *C Plant*

Bottom right: Although the Southern Region does not have an allocation of Class 47 locomotives they nevertheless work through to Southern Region destinations with both freight and passenger trains. No 47 238 eases round the sharp curve at Salisbury with a Yeoman stone train from Merehead Quarry near Witham, and passes SR Class 205 three-car diesel-electric unit No 1101 waiting in the bay on 18 September 1975.   *G T Heavyside*

The difference in level between the up and down Severn Tunnel lines near Patchway is quite clear in this photograph of No 47 506 seen here approaching Patchway with the 07.50 Swansea–Paddington on 6 July 1974. Partly obscuring the third coach is the advance warning indicator for the permanent speed restriction through Patchway Junction, which shows the speed limit figures on the face of the disc, and is accompanied by an automatic warning system caution magnet. The difference in level of the tracks here arises from the fact that the down line, the upper one in the photograph with the freight train disappearing in the distance, was the original single track branch to Severn Beach, in existence before the Severn Tunnel was built. When the tunnel route was opened the line was doubled but in order to give the heavy coal trains an easier route the new up line was built with even gradients throughout compared with the short steep gradients of the down line and the two lines are on different levels between Pilning and Patchway. *P J Fowler*

Above: When occasion arises Class 47s can also be used for shunting, although they are not an ideal locomotive for this use. No 47 214 marshals a long freight at Warrington Arpley on 28 July 1976. *K Connolly*

Top right: Not a distortion in the photograph but the church spire at Chesterfield really is crooked. Approaching No 47 350 meets an unidentified Class 47, both with expresses to and from St Pancras on 10 July 1976.
G T Heavyside

Right: Landore-based Class 47 No 47 495 takes the high speed junction at Severn Tunnel Junction to head for the Tunnel with the 08.45 Swansea–Paddington on 14 June 1974. In the background is a line-up of locomotives waiting to work freights out of Severn Tunnel Junction yard.
Barry J Nicolle

Above: Class 47s work many trains in Scotland although their activities do not normally extend north of Perth and Aberdeen over Highland lines. No 47 206 leaves Perth with the 13.20 Aberdeen–Kings Cross on 28 August 1976. *K Connolly*

Top left: Breasting the 1 in 37 at the summit of the Lickey incline is No 47 177 heading for Birmingham with a train from the West of England on 26 April 1975.

D E Canning

Left: One of the named Class 47s, No 47 079, originally 1664, *George Jackson Churchward*, accelerates from Cheltenham Spa on the Birmingham–Bristol line with a block load of oil tank empties on 30 May 1974. The pair of tracks in the background formed the freight route to Birmingham via Stratford-on-Avon. *Barry J Nicolle*

Above: Some of the Class 47s are fitted with special controls to allow running at very slow speeds on merry-go-round trains where coal hopper wagons are hauled through unloading and loading plants on the move. In theory the trains never stop and are always on a continuous working between, for example, collieries and power stations, although only a few locations in fact operate merry-go-round trains in this fashion. Here No 47 321 approaches Toton yard with empty merry-go-round hopper wagons on 7 June 1975.   *Rev Graham B Wise*

Top left: A Class 47 heads the daytime motorail train from Kensington Olympia to Perth which runs down the Midland main line on the Settle & Carlisle route; it is seen here crossing Batty Moss viaduct in September 1971.
Stanley Creer

Left: A Class 47 arrives at Tyne yard from the Newcastle direction with a block load of ICI four-wheel tank wagons containing chemicals. At the front and back of the tank wagons are special barrier wagons provided to absorb shocks in the unlikely event of an accident.
G T Heavyside

Above: Class 47 locomotives work the principal trains in East Anglia between Liverpool Street and Norwich; No 47 156 is seen leaving Liverpool Street with the 16.30 for Norwich on a very wet 2 October 1975.   *G T Heavyside*

Left: A Class 47, still carrying its original number 1748, accelerates from Ipswich with a Liverpool Street–Norwich express on 15 October 1973.   *J D Mann*

Above: The catenary had already been erected down the GN main line in the London area ready for the suburban electrification from Kings Cross and Moorgate as Class 47 No 47 416 passes Hadley Wood with the Saturday 11.45 Kings Cross—Newcastle on 24 May 1975.　*Kevin Lane*

Below: From the building of the East Coast main line until 1973 Peterborough station was situated on a sharp reverse curve which meant that all non-stopping trains had to slow to 15mph through the station. Although room was available to realign the tracks this was not done until a few years ago when a new down side platform was built and fast lines rebuilt on a much easier alignment, which allowed non-stopping trains to pass at 100mph. Here Class 47 No 47 413 leaves the new down platform at Peterborough with the 10.15 Kings Cross—Leeds on 2 May 1975.　*G T Heavyside*

bove: Another location where speed used to be limited, though only to 70mph, was Offord, near Huntingdon, ˙here the railway followed the curves of the River Ouse. ˙art of the civil engineering works carried out on the East ˙oast main line to ease speed limits where possible in-˙uded a realignment of the river bank and the railway at ˙fford to remove the speed restriction completely. No 47 ˙46 passes Offord Cluny with the 13.00 Kings ˙oss–Edinburgh on 1 May 1975. *G T Heavyside*

Below: The approach to Peterborough from the north with No 47 045 heading a load of hopper wagons carrying fly ash on 2 May 1975. The two tracks on the left are those from March to Leicester. *G T Heavyside*

4 THE CLASS 40s— BR's DIESEL VETERANS

The English Electric Class 40s, characterised by their very long bodies and eight-wheel bogies, were the first main line locomotives for Inter-city passenger work and were originally used on services from Liverpool Street, Kings Cross and Euston. They were heavy locomotives, and with a top speed of 90mph were at a slight disadvantage compared with the later types of diesel with more power and able to run at slightly higher speeds. Gradually they lost their place on principal Inter-city work but today still find employment on certain routes and particularly on freight in North East and North West England.

Above left: One of the early batches of Class 40s, some of which retain their original headcode discs and corridor doors, is No 40 031, seen here standing at Blackpool North with a Glasgow and Edinburgh train. To the right sister locomotive No 40 017, formerly named *Carinthia*, waits to work a train to Manchester on 31 July 1976.
K Connolly

Left: Class 40s are also active on the various trans-Pennine routes and No 40 032 approaches Huddersfield with the 10.10 Liverpool—Newcastle on 24 July 1976.
G T Heavyside

Above: Much of the express passenger work on the North Wales coast line between Crewe, Llandudno and Holyhead is in the hands of Class 40s; No 319 is seen leaving Chester with a Bangor—Euston train on 16 June 1972.
C Plant

Above: Class 40s are still active on the East Coast main line and allied services, although not normally on top-line express work which needs the added power of the Class 47s or Class 55s. Here No 40 172 leaves York with a Scarborough to Edinburgh train on 2 August 1975.

K Connolly

Below: Another of the early Class 40s, this one No 40 006, leaves Tyne yard bound for the Newcastle direction with a train of empty ballast hopper wagons.

G T Heavyside

Above: Some of the Class 40s received the one piece four-character headcode panels but with a further change of policy the panels are now out of use and the locomotives will revert to headlight fittings, although merely to denote warning of approach rather than the class of train. Here No 40 186 passes the freightliner depot at Portobello Edinburgh with an up freightliner service on 16 June 1976.
G T Heavyside

Below: Newcastle Central has basically changed little in its general appearance since steam days but no longer do electric trains leave the right-hand platforms bound for Whitley Bay and the Northumberland coast, but the castle keep overlooking the tracks still gives this splendid vantage point as Class 40 No 280 leaves Newcastle with a train for Edinburgh on 2 September 1972.
G T Heavyside

5 PEAKS TO THE NORTH AND TO THE WEST

The first ten locomotives built by British Railways with Sulzer diesel engines, now Class 44, carried the names of mountain peaks in England and Wales and the designation Peak is associated by many enthusiasts with all the locomotives of Classes 44, 45 and 46, even though some Class 45s are named after regiments. Like the Brush Sulzer Class 47s the Peaks can be found in many parts of the country, particularly on the Midland main line from St Pancras to the North, and on North and West services between North East England, Birmingham, South Wales and South West England. At the time of writing, passengers in South West England, west of Taunton can almost tell their destination by the class of locomotive. If it is a Class 45 or 46 then it will almost certainly be bound for Bristol, Birmingham and the North and if a Class 47 or 50 then it is for London. There are though the exceptions!

Above: The photographer is just 121 miles from Derby by the former Midland main line towards Bristol but this section is now no more than a siding running south from Yate. Birmingham line trains from Bristol now use the former Great Western route via Filton Junction and the London line as far as Westerleigh Junction where they fork left to join the original Midland line at Yate. An unidentified Class 45 with the 10.25 Penzance–Leeds is about to leave the South Wales–London line at Westerleigh to turn north towards Birmingham on 31 March 1975.
Brian Edwards

Right: Another unidentified Class 45 is seen at the head of the 07.38 Plymouth–Edinburgh on the former Midland main line between Charfield and Berkeley Road on 28 March 1975. In the background is the Tyndale monument at North Nibley.
Brian Edwards

Top left: The Class 45s and 46s are very active on the WR in the West of England, mostly on workings involving trains between Birmingham and either South Wales or the West Country or locally on fill-in duties. A Class 45 is seen here passing Bristol Temple Meads with a train carrying paper pulp from Portishead to St Annes board mill near Marsh Junction, Bristol. *P J Fowler*

Bottom left: At the foot of the Lickey Incline No 45 001 passes Bromsgrove with the 08.30 Manchester–Swansea on 14 June 1975. In steam days the sidings bottom left would have been the standing point for the Lickey Incline banking engines waiting for their next turn of duty. *J G Glover*

Above: Some years ago the Western Region rebuilt the original Brunel bridge over the River Wye at Chepstow but the new girder structure is equally impressive. A Class 45 heads the 14.24 Manchester Piccadilly to Cardiff across the bridge on 11 May 1973. *P J Fowler*

Below: The steep South Devon banks do not hold as much terror for today's diesels as they did in steam days but even so it is often a steady slog up the 1 in 37 of the steepest parts of the climb over Dainton summit. Class 45 No 15 storms the western slope of Dainton bank at the head of the up Cornishman from Penzance to Leeds on 21 July 1970. *G F Gillham*

Above: Class 45s are staple power on the Midland main line from St Pancras and on the few passenger workings that continue north over the Settle & Carlisle line between Leeds, Carlisle and onwards via the Glasgow & South Western route to Glasgow. No 45 036 waits at Carlisle with the 11.39 to Glasgow on 26 July 1976. *K Connolly*

Below: Equally at home on passenger or freight work No 45 042 is seen here with a down coal train leaving Ampthill Tunnel between Flitwick and Bedford on 29 April 1975. Until traffic flows were altered on British Railways some years ago this would have almost been like carrying coal to Newcastle, for on the Midland main line in steam days loaded coal trains always worked up towards London and empties worked north. *G T Heavyside*

Above: Clay Cross South Junction is the meeting point of two principal Inter-city routes, the one on the right from Birmingham and Derby which carries a large number of trains between the South West of England, South Wales and the North East, also certain trains from St Pancras to Sheffield and beyond which travel via Derby; the lines curving round to the left form the direct route to Trent and Leicester, and also Nottingham. Class 46 No 46 085 approaches off the Derby line with a train towards Sheffield on 10 July 1976.   *G T Heavyside*

Below: With a newly modified front end, including head-lamps instead of a four-character headcode panel, No 45 063 arrives at Derby with the 10.12 Newcastle–Cardiff train on 10 July 1976.   *K Connolly*

6 THE CLASS 50s—BR's LAST EXPRESS LOCOMOTIVES?

The Class 50s were built originally by English Electric and intended for working in pairs on principal expresses between Crewe, Carlisle and Glasgow in the late 1960s to give times and top speeds of 100mph comparable with the electric service south of Crewe. Once the West Coast main line had been electrified between Crewe and Glas-

gow in 1974 most of the Class 50s were transferred to the Western Region. With future BR high-speed passenger services in the hands of Inter-city 125 units, the Class 50s could well be the last locomotives designed for express passenger working.

Top: Although most Class 50s were transferred to the Western Region after electrification of the West Coast main line between Crewe and Glasgow, some were retained by the London Midland Region for working freight services over the Settle & Carlisle line where No 50 012 is seen just south of Appleby on 18 June 1975.

G T Heavyside

bove: Three trains in a row with a Class 50 leaving Bristol emple Meads heading a train for Paddington via Badmin-on running neck-and-neck with a three-car diesel multi-le-unit bound for Cardiff. Between them an oil train asses in the opposite direction headed by a Class 52 ocomotive.

P J Fowler

Bottom: No 50 021 stands at Birmingham New Street after arrival with the 16.05 from Paddington on 26 November 1976. Some WR crews started the practice of displaying the locomotive number as near as possible in the route indicator panel on both these and the Class 52 locomotives.

K Connolly

Left: Class 50 meets Class 50 at Bath in the winter of 1976. *P J Fowler*

Bottom left: Class 50 047 accelerates with the 10.15 Paddington—Bristol past Paddington goods station soon after leaving the terminus on 1 November 1975. On the right Class 47 No 47 497 runs light towards Paddington to work the 10.30 to Paignton. *K Connolly*

Below: A few Paddington—West of England services call at Castle Cary but Class 50 No 50 014 passes through non-stop with the 15.30 Paddington—Penzance on 28 May 1975. *K Connolly*

THE WESTERNS' LAST FLING

st as this book was in preparation the Western Class 52 comotives were working out their final days before complete withdrawal. In the last few months there were the evitable enthusiast excursions, even the sight of a Western Class diesel working out of Kings Cross to York.

p left: Easily matching the best of steam locomotive hausts but not really the thing for a diesel to do, Class 52 1016 *Western Gladiator* makes a spectacular start out Exeter having just taken over the 07.40 eds–Penzance following the failure of a Class 47 hich had brought the train in on 8 September 1975.
K Connolly

ottom left: London Transport's Metropolitan line to ammersmith passes under the WR main lines between yal Oak and Westbourne Park. Class 52 No 1064 *estern Regent* accelerates across the flyunder with the .20 Paddington–Penzance on 23 August 1975.
K Connolly

Above: One of the regular duties of the Class 52s, particularly in the last few years of their life, was to work the stone trains from Merehead Quarry on the branch from Witham. No 1016 *Western Gladiator* drifts forward from the branch into the goods loop at Witham to await a path out on to the main line towards Westbury. *K Connolly*

Below: A Western in the far West with No 1022 *Western Sentinel* at Penzance with the 11.00 to Paddington on 1 April 1975. *K Connolly*

Above: Front end contrast between Class 52 No 1049 *Western Monarch* on the left and Class 50 No 50 007 on the right which has just arrived with the 06.45 from Penzance to Paddington. *K Connolly*

Top right: Another duty on which Westerns were frequently employed were the china clay trains from Cornwall; No 1053 *Western Patriarch* passes Lostwithiel with empty china clay wagons bound for Par on 14 July 197▯ *K Connol▯*

Bottom right: Not an optical illusion but really a Class 5▯ No 1023 *Western Fusilier*, at Kings Cross on 2▯ November 1976 with an enthusiast special for York. O▯ the far side of the station Class 55 No 55 008 *The Gree▯ Howards* waits to leave with the 09.00 to Newcastle. N▯ 1023 is seen here with the new white spot headlamps ▯ place of its four-character route indicator, the first Clas▯ 52 to be so fitted and in view of their imminent withdraw▯ at that time probably the only one. Two members of th▯ class have been preserved on the Torbay line of the Da▯ Valley Railway. *K Connol.*

8 ELECTRICS TO THE SOUTH COAST

The Southern electric system is complex and covers practically all routes between London and the Kent and Sussex coasts and as far west as Bournemouth. With electrification completed on the various main lines at different periods each has been provided with different batches of stock, incorporating new design ideas or latest technical improvements so that there is considerable variety in Southern electric units.

The development of Southern Region express electric stock; *Top left:* the 4CEP units, one of which is seen leading this train from Victoria to Littlehampton at Redhill, followed very much the layout of the old Southern Railway 4COR units originally built for Waterloo-Portsmouth services. The coaches of the CEP stock were of BR standard design with an open motor brake second at each end of the unit and composite and second class coaches in the middle. *Bottom left:* The new BR express electric stock for the Brighton line introduced in 1964 had only one motor coach in the middle of a four-car unit and driving trailer coaches at each end. The IG in the CIG code for these units was the old telegraphic code for Brighton, although today these units can be found on both Brighton and Portsmouth main lines. Unit No 7366 leads the 09.45 Brighton-Victoria at Keymer Junction on 28 April 1971. The tracks

going off to the left are to Lewes, Eastbourne and Hastings. *Below:* Express electrics on the Bournemouth main line follow an entirely different concept since because of operational needs these trains work push-pull. The four coaches nearest the camera in this photograph form a powered unit with a motor coach at each end, classified 4REP by the Southern, and Class 430 in the now standard numerical code. The other eight coaches in the train are formed of two four-car unpowered units equipped with driving cabs at each end so that the driver can control the train from the leading cab. The train is pushed from Waterloo to Bournemouth by the four-car powered unit which terminates at Bournemouth, but the unpowered units are then diesel-hauled on to Weymouth, and propelled back as far as Bournemouth for the return journey where they are once again coupled to an electric 4REP set.

J Scrace (2) G T Heavyside

Above: Southern Region inner suburban services in the London area are generally worked by four-car electric units differing in a number of details but all broadly similar in concept. This is 4EPB unit No 5160 of Class 415 seen here at Denmark Hill working the 13.30 Sevenoaks to Holborn Viaduct on 11 August 1970.   *J Scrace*

Top right: New look for Southern Region suburban stock with the prototype 4PEP units 4001/2 of Class 445, seen arriving at Thames Ditton on a Hampton Court-Waterloo working on 1 October 1973. These units which have been undergoing trials on the Southern are the first on that region to have sliding doors and have served as prototypes for the new electric trains on the Moorgate-Welwyn Garden City and Hertford suburban lines of the Eastern Region.   *J Scrace*

Right: Latest outer suburban trains on the Southern are similar to the inner suburban type with side doors to each set of seats but have corridors through the train and toilet facilities. They are used on the longer distance stopping services from London to the coast or intermediately. 4VEP unit No 7772 working the 14.06 service from Victoria to Bognor Regis on 26 April 1973 is seen leaving Gatwick Airport station, which is directly linked with the airport terminal buildings.   *J Scrace*

Left: The original outer suburban units on Kent Coast lines were basically little different from some ordinary inner suburban stock but one coach in each pair of the two-car units included toilet facilities, although there was no through corridor between the coaches. Here 2HAP unit No 6040, now known as Class 414, leaves Dartford on the 13.45 Ramsgate-Charing Cross service on 1 September 1970. Since then several of these units have been relegated to purely suburban work and regraded as second class only. *J Scrace*

Above: Study in carriage roofs at Clapham Junction carriage sidings on 28 April 1976. Most of the vehicles on the left are locomotive-hauled coaches, those on the right are multiple-units. *Rev Graham B Wise*

Top left: The electric locomotives built for the Kent Coast electrification in 1959 were equipped for taking current both from the third rail used on all SR running lines, and from overhead catenary in yards and sidings where a third rail would be dangerous to staff working on the ground. Here is an unusual shot of locomotive No 71 008 working under power from the catenary with its pantograph up at Snowdown colliery sidings, in Kent, about to leave with coal for Workington steel works in Cumberland on 17 September 1974. Later Southern electric locomotives have been built as electro-diesels with a small diesel engine to provide power for working on non-electrified lines and have made the pure electric locomotives seem rather inflexible; at the end of 1976 the Class 71 locomotives were taken out of traffic and stored while their duties were taken over by electro-diesel types. *G T Heavyside*

Left: A Class 73 electro-diesel, here still retaining its original number E6002, heads the 12.04 Chichester-Norwood Junction freight near Horsham on 4 May 1973. *J Scrace*

Above: When steam locomotives came to an end on the Isle of Wight Ryde-Shanklin line in 1966 the Southern Region electrified it on the third rail system, but, because of restricted clearances at overbridges and stations, could not use standard Southern electric coaches since they were too big. The Southern therefore acquired redundant London Transport Underground trains for working on the Island and adapted them for third rail working. They were formed into four and three-car units, coded 4VEC and 3TIS from Vectis, the Latin name of the Isle of Wight. Here a seven-car train, led by unit 035, leaves Brading for Shanklin on 22 June 1974. *J Scrace*

9 MIXED TRAFFIC

This section portrays some of the smaller locomotives, the lower-power mixed traffic types which never seem to attract the limelight like their more powerful sisters which handle most of the express work. Yet the mixed-traffic diesels are capable of use on practically all types of trains, even 90 mile an hour running with moderately loaded passenger trains. If more power is wanted two can be coupled together and worked in multiple under the control of one driver, and in the Highlands of Scotland the Class 25s, 26s and 27s are staple power on all services. The Scottish region even developed its own form of multiple-unit working with a locomotive at each end of a six-car train for high-speed Inter-city services between Edinburgh and Glasgow.

Left: One of the English Electric maid-of-all work diesels Class 37 No 37 054 approaches Blackpool North with a summer Saturday train from Leicester on 31 July 1976. This locomotive is one of the earlier batch which had split train headcode indicators on each side of the gangway doors. *K Connolly*

Bottom left: A general view of Tinsley marshalling yard near Sheffield, with Class 37 No 37 124 approaching the reception sidings with a coal train for marshalling on 16 July 1976. The locomotive on the left is one of the three specially adapted master and slave diesel-electric shunters of Class 13 used in Tinsley yard. Each pair were originally two separate locomotives; one was stripped of its cab and driver's controls and it works under the command of the master locomotive nearer the camera. *G T Heavyside*

Below: Class 37s are active in South Wales, particularly on freight services. No 37 225 joins the Newport–Cardiff main line at Ebbw Junction with coal from the Western Valleys on 26 March 1976. *G T Heavyside*

The Southern Region's Class 33 locomotives are versatile machines, and as a diesel class are unusual in being allocated entirely to one region. They cover freight and a few passenger workings throughout the Region, and some of the class are fitted for push-pull working in conjunction with SR multiple-unit stock. As such, they work the Bournemouth–Weymouth leg (*above*) of the through Waterloo–Weymouth service with the unpowered 4TC four-car units, which are electrically-worked between Bournemouth and Waterloo by 4REP units. *Top left:* No 33 029 is seen on an inter-regional freight service heading the 10.00 Northampton–Fawley empty oil tanks near Hounslow on 28 August 1974. *J Scrace. Left:* No 33 048 rounds the head of Southampton Water and approaches Totton with an inter-regional passenger train from the North of England to Bournemouth on 20 September 1975. This train would have worked through via Reading and Basingstoke to reach Southern Region territory.

G T Heavyside

Below: The Class 31 locomotives were originally built primarily for the Eastern Region and are unusual in that although having six-wheel bogies only two axles out of the three on each bogie are powered. As originally designed in 1957 they were fitted with Mirrlees, Bickerton & Day diesel engines rated at 1,250hp but in later years they were rebuilt with English Electric 1,470hp engines. Some were later transferred to the Western Region to replace withdrawn diesel-hydraulic types. No 31 224 is seen here climbing away from Kings Cross between Gasworks and Copenhagen Tunnels in August 1975 with a Cambridge train. Work is seen in progress here on track alterations in connection with the suburban electrification into Kings Cross. The bridge over the East Coast main line carries the North London line, an important cross—London freight route. *J G Glover*

Right: The Manchester—Sheffield—Wath route, electrified on the overhead system at 1500Vdc, is virtually unseen by the public for it no longer carries regular passenger traffic and is today used only by freight over much of its length. As a result the small class of Co-Co electric locomotives built in 1954 for passenger working were later sold to the Netherlands Railways, which uses the same electrical system, but the Bo-Bo locomotives remain on freight working, of which No 76 053 here passes Torside, climbing towards Woodhead tunnel with coal empties on 22 July 1976. *G T Heavyside*

Bottom right: A Class 31 on the Western Region with No 31 112 heading a Weymouth-Bristol train seen taking the Westbury station loop at Fairwood Junction on 4 June 1976. *K Connolly*

Above: Although the original English Electric Type 1 loco-motives, now known as Class 20, were used on both freight and a few local passenger workings in certain areas, their passenger appearances today are now very rare, although they may be used on empty stock trains and for station pilot duties. Here a pair of Class 20s, still with their original numbers 8088 and 8155, pass Derby with a train of empty coal hoppers on 13 September 1972.

C Plant

Right: The BR/Sulzer Type 2 now known as classes 2 and 25 are used widely on freight duties and also secon ary passenger work. Here No 25 048 approaches Fro sham on the Warrington—Chester line with empty tanks for Ellesmere Port on 9 August 1975. The waterw in the foreground is part of the Weaver Navigation.

G T Heavysi

Below: No 20 011 draws into Glasgow Central with the empty stock for the up West Coast Postal for Euston on 23 May 1974.

G T Heavyside

Left: No 25 050 heads a down freight just north of Culgaith on the Settle & Carlisle line on 20 June 1975.

G T Heavyside

Bottom left: One of the older members of the Class, No 24 063, shunts at Croes Newydd Junction, just south of Wrexham General Station, on 12 July 1976. With the decline in freight traffic during 1975 and 1976 many locomotives in Class 24 were taken out of service and stored.

G T Heavyside

Below: On the Highland lines in Scotland, north of Perth and Aberdeen, practically all services are in the hands of what used to be known as Type 2 locomotives, that is today's Classes 24, 25, 26 and 27, although towards the end of 1976 most of the Class 24 locomotives had been taken out of service. No 24 124, however, was still active on 4 July 1975 with a ballast train on the very bleak and remote West Highland line at Rannoch. *John Goss*

Above: 'Skye? Just across there'. Class 24 No 5118 stands at Kyle of Lochalsh after arrival with the midday train from Inverness on 11 October 1973.   *P J Fowler*

Top right: When the diesel multiple-units on the service between Glasgow and Edinburgh were beginning to prove unequal to the task the Scottish Region formed their own 'high-speed trains' by using Mark 2 Inter-city coaches, surplus from other main lines, formed into six-car trains with a Class 27 locomotive marshalled at each end and connected to run in multiple. Thus they had all the operating advantages of a multiple-unit but without the mu's inflexibility in that the locomotives can be detached from the coaches for maintenance and repair, or for other duties when the Glasgow–Edinburgh passenger service is not running. These trains are able to run up to 90mph on this service and brought new fast timings. Here No 27 202 at the leading end and 27 101 at the back, arrive at Falkirk Grahamston with the 14.00 Glasgow Central–Edinburgh on 29 August 1976. This was a special Sunday diversion, for the normal route is via Falkirk High, and at the Glasgow end these trains normally use Queen Street rather than Central.   *G T Heavyside*

Bottom right: The Class 26 and 27 locomotives were originally built by the Birmingham Railway Carriage & Wagon Company with Sulzer diesel engines, the main detail differences between them being the Crompton Parkinson electrical equipment on the former and GEC electrical equipment on the latter. Here No 26 007 heads up the East Coast main line at Prestonpans with a coal train for Cockenzie power station on 16 June 1976.

G T Heavyside

Top left: Many of the heavier trains on Highland lines are double headed by pairs of Type 2 locomotives. Here the 17.40 Oban to Glasgow Queen Street leaves Crianlarich Junction behind Class 27 Nos 27 016 and 27 009 on 5 September 1976. *K Connolly*

Bottom left: No 27 035 leaves Crianlarich Junction and passes the memorial gardens with a Glasgow-Mallaig train on 5 September 1976. *K Connolly*

Above: The West Highland line between Glasgow and Fort William, together with the extension to Mallaig, passes through some spectacular Highland scenery. Moreover when the West Highland Extension railway was built around the turn of the century between Fort William and Mallaig the contractors, Robert McAlpine & Sons, made extensive use of concrete for many of the civil engineering features, the first major application on such a scale in the world. Among the concrete constructions was Glenfinnan Viaduct, seen here with the 12.09 Mallaig-Fort William train on 2 July 1975. *John Goss*

0 MULTIPLE-UNIT VARIETY

Many suburban, branch and main line stopping services on non-electrified lines are worked by diesel multiple-units, which come in an extraordinary variety of types ranging from non-corridor compartment coaches to a similar type with through gangways, right up to coaches of main line corridor standards for longer distance work. This section features stock of varying ages and shows the remarkable variations in front end design to try and get away from the box on wheels styles of the 1950s.

At the end of the 1950s the BR design panel made a positive attempt to improve the general appearance and outlook of the front ends of diesel and electric multiple-units. The wrap-round windscreen and curved front ends improved matters and gave an attractive appearance provided it was kept clean. However, more recent designs, particularly the new electric multiple-units for Kings Cross-Hitchin and Royston services, have reverted to flat front ends and windows, because of the danger of splintered glass if an obstruction hits the wrap-round type of windscreen. Flat windows can be made of much tougher glass to resist impacts. *Top left:* Two three-car AC electric multiple-units on Glasgow suburban work stand at Springburn on 6 March 1976. *Bottom left:* The Trans-Pennine diesel multiple-units had a similar front end to the Glasgow units, above, although differing in detail. Here a five-car, forming the 11.47 Hull–Liverpool, heads west near Mirfield on 13 July 1976. On the left is the site of the former Mirfield locomotive depot. *Above:* One of the Swindon-built Inter-city type dmus of Class 123, which can be marshalled in either three or four-car units. The front end design was varied slightly on these units to accommodate a through gangway. Here two three-car units approach Marshbrook level crossing between Craven Arms and Church Stretton working the 11.35 Cardiff–Crewe on 17 July 1976.   *G T Heavyside* (all)

Above: Many of the Southern Region diesel-electric multiple-units are formed of suburban type coaches with side doors, although one coach in each unit has toilets and first class accommodation. Despite the rather spartan type of accommodation these units are used on some long distance services, including Portsmouth–Bristol. Three-car unit No 1104 takes the Romsey line at Tunnel Junction just outside Salisbury, where it leaves the main line to Waterloo, on a Salisbury-Portsmouth working on 18 September 1975. *G T Heavyside*

Top left: The Tonbridge–Hastings line of the Southern Region has required special stock for many years because of restricted clearances through some of the tunnels on the line which precludes the use of normal width stock. To replace steam locomotives on the line in 1957 the Southern built six-car units with a diesel-electric motor coach at each end and corridors through the train. Some of the units include buffet cars. The first few units were built on the shorter 56ft 11in underframes instead of the 63ft 5in underframes on most other BR stock. Here one of the short units, No 1001, on the 14.40 Charing Cross–Hastings service, leaves Robertsbridge on 5 September 1969. *J Scrace*

Left: Two WR three car cross-country diesel multiple-unit sets head towards Cardiff working the 09.06 service from Bristol Temple Meads on 6 July 1974; they are seen here soon after passing Patchway where the Severn Tunnel main line is on two levels as described on page 25. *P J Fowler*

Above: The meanderings of the Western Region line between Westbury, Trowbridge, Bradford-on-Avon and Bath are clearly seen in this view near Freshford where the line runs along the Avon valley. In the background is Dundas Aqueduct. A three-car SR diesel-electric unit on a Bristol–Portsmouth service is approaching in the foreground on 17 November 1974.   *P J Fowler*

Top right: One of the most unusual types of diesel multiple-units are the six 'Tadpole' units formed by the Southern Region for working between Reading, Guildford, Redhill and Tonbridge. The leading driving trailer coach was formerly part of an electric unit while the two coaches at the back were part of a Hastings line six-car corridor unit. Because of the different widths of the coaches, they acquired their nickname but they are now known as Class 206. Unit No 1205 leaves Guildford on 4 November 1968.   *J Scrace*

Right: The line between Tonbridge and Tunbridge Well on the Hastings line includes some tunnels which restric the width of coaches but not so tight as one tunnel furthe south near Mountfield Halt. Nevertheless, because a num ber of branch services in East Sussex, dieselised in th early 1960s, worked into Tonbridge, they required speci stock 8ft 6in wide. One of these East Sussex units of Clas 207 is seen at Honor Oak Park on a London Bridge-Erid working on 20 April 1969. The black triangle on the fro of the train indicates that the guards van and parcels a commodation is at the front of the unit, as a warning station staff.   *J Scrac*

Top right: Now that some of the diesel multiple-units on BR are between 10 and 20 years old a refurbishing programme is being undertaken on units which it is considered will have a longer term future. The units have improved seating, new brightly-coloured interiors and different external livery consisting of the pale grey body colour normally used on the upper panels of Inter-city stock, with a broad blue line beneath the windows and the yellow front end. Here a refurbished unit stands at York waiting to leave for Harrogate on 1 November 1975.

D E Canning

Below: One of the two-car diesel multiple-units built by Park Royal is seen here at Blaenau Ffestiniog on the branch working from Llandudno on 31 May 1973.

J Scrace

Bottom right: Two pairs of Metropolitan-Cammell diesel multiple-units arrive at Portmadoc on a working from Pwllheli to Machynlleth on 30 August 1972.   *J Scrace*

Top left: A diesel service which ceased just as this book was in preparation was that between Kings Cross and Hertford, where for many years Cravens two-car units had maintained most services. From November 1976 new electric trains took over the services, working through to Moorgate from Finsbury Park. A two-car diesel unit is seen under the newly-erected catenary approaching Crews Hill on the Hertford North line on 16 September 1974.

D Griffiths

Bottom left: Suburban services in different parts of the country are worked by varying types of unit. In South Wales they are mostly three-car units of stock with side doors, as are many WR services. Here a six-car train forming the 09.50 Merthyr–Barry Island arrives at Abercynon on 26 March 1976. The line disappearing to the left is that to Aberdare; from here down the valley the line becomes double track.

G T Heavyside

Below: Two three-car diesel multiple-units, originally built by the Birmingham Railway Carriage & Wagon Co, leave Bolton Trinity Street forming the 18.10 Blackpool North–Manchester Victoria working on 4 June 1976. To improve the appearance of these units some have been given broad grey bands beneath the windows to relieve the otherwise all-over blue livery.

G T Heavyside

Above: Single-car diesel multiple-units are used on a number of branch services but also on one or two main line stopping services including this Reading-Bedwyn duty, seen here at Hungerford on 30 July 1976.

P J Fowler

Left: Single unit and single railway enthusiast; a one-car diesel unit approaches Ashley Hill, Bristol, on a Severn Beach–Temple Meads working in April 1974.

P J Fowler

Below: Two-car diesel multiple-units work many services in East Anglia and South Lincolnshire. The 10.34 Doncaster–Cambridge slows to take the right-hand route at Sleaford North Junction to reach Sleaford station on 8 October 1976.

G T Heavyside

A WR three-car cross-country unit working the 09.08 Bristol-Portsmouth on 1 May 1976 is framed by trees above the River Avon as it leaves Bradford-on-Avon.

P J Fowler

1 HIGH-SPEED FUTURE

ter-city 125 units, designed to run continuously where
ack conditions permit at 200km/hr (125mph), entered
rvice from Paddington to South Wales and Bristol in
ctober 1976. The photographs here show the sleek lines
these units and in particular the streamlined front end
hich makes these units look so impressive.

ove: One of the Western Region Inter-City 125
its speeds past the camera on its way from London to
stol and *top left* another arrives at Bristol Temple
ads working the 16.00 Weston-super-Mare–
ddington in October 1976.　　　　　*P J Fowler*

ttom left: The prototype HST set, with its reversed
ery, is seen here during trial runs between London and
istol leaving Box tunnel in May 1975.　　　*G F Heiron*

Left: Old and new at Temple Meads on 5 November 1976 with, on the left, Class 52 No 1013 *Western Ranger* waiting to work the 08.00 Bristol to Penzance, and on the right an Inter-city 125 set arriving on the 06.48 Taunton–Paddington via Bristol Parkway. *P J Fowler*

Below left & right: The striking front end of Inter-city 125 units; Nos 253 003 and 253 005 at Bristol Temple Meads in October 1976. *P J Fowler*

An IC 125 train speeds along the Badminton route between Bristol and Paddington near Great Somerford on 31 October 1976.   *P J Fowler*